Snogging

Snogging

A Beginner's Guide to The Art of Kissing

by
Simon Mayo and Martin Wroe

"A LIP-SMACKING, TONGUE-WAGGLiNG, TOOTH-CRACKING, LOVE-BITING MEGA-SNOG OF A BOOK..."
Snog Hits Magazine

HarperCollins*Publishers*

Acknowledgements
Photographs of Jakki Brambles, p44, Gary Davies, p54,
Caron Keating, p26, Philip Schofield, p36, and Steve Wright, p13,
all courtesy of James Grant Group of Companies.

First published in Great Britain in 1992 by
HarperCollins*Publishers*
77-85 Fulham Palace Road, Hammersmith,
London W6 8JB

ISBN 0 551 02425 9

Printed and bound in Great Britain by
Scotprint Limited

A catalogue record for this book is
available from the British Library

Contents

1

Kissing Slang: Some Words You Should Look Out For

Words and phrases you will come across in the course of your kissing activities. Use it as a vocabulary checklist. Champion snoggers might want to see how many they can get in on the same date - but never use the same one twice on the same night.

Snog	❑
Kiss	❑
Lip-smacker	❑
Suck-face	❑
Gob-smacker	❑
Lip-enhancement	❑
Lip-injection	❑
Lippy	❑
Hit	❑
Smacker	❑

Tongue-Sushi	❑
Chew-Face	❑
Mug	❑
Swap-Spit	❑
Kiss me Quick	❑
Kissed Off	❑
Seriously Kissed Off	❑
Tongue-Sandwich	❑
Oral Hijinks	❑
Kiss and Make-Up	❑

Kiss and Break Up	❑
Kissy Kissy	❑
Holy Kiss	❑
Saliva-Selecta	❑
Kissing to be Clever	❑
Kiss it Better, There, There	❑
Lip-Champer	❑
Ulcerator	❑

Lip-smacking, thirst-quenching…	❑
Watch your lip…	❑
Kiss of Life	❑
Kiss of Death	❑
French Kissing	❑
Kiss and Cuddle, Slap and Tickle	❑

> **In a kiss two spirits meet, mingle and become one; and as a result there arises in the mind a wonderful feeling of delight that awakens and binds together the love of them that kiss.**
> **St Aelred of Rievaulx**

A husband out for the evening without his wife's knowledge was saved from death by a terrorist gunman when he leant over to kiss his lover. The lucky escape happened when the man, enjoying an illicit meeting with his girlfriend in his car, leaned over for a snog, and a bullet fired at him passed through the car window shattering the windscreen. That'll teach him.

Authors' Note:

In this book it is her who is being asked out, she who is the beautiful blossom of desire ... this is because the authors are two happily married men. You may find, for example, if you are of the female sexual persuasion, that you need to do the odd piece of quick sexual translation - so that the illustration in question fits your own unique romantic situation. Thank you for your patience. Now read on.

2
Fancying Someone

How You Can Tell

Imagine you are walking down a crowded high street alone with your thoughts. A girl comes up to you and says, "Cedric, I can't go on without telling you this, life is becoming unbearable, this morning I nearly slashed my wrists, I've got to have you, I need you, I'm a desperate woman ... I love you, I love you, I love you." She then throws herself at your feet, clutching your ankles, as the passing shoppers look on in bewilderment and not a little disgust.

You can be fairly certain that the young woman in question has taken a liking to you, she finds you attractive, she is prepared to spend her life with you. In short, she fancies you.

But, in many instances, whether a person of the opposite sex fancies you may not be quite as easy to tell as it was for Cedric in our wholly true and authentic illustration.

Perhaps you think you catch her eye across a crowded dance floor. But perhaps she is cross-eyed. And anyway it is pitch-black - how can you be sure?

> **Groucho Marx was once caught kissing a showgirl by his wife. He protested: "Kissing her? I was only whispering in her mouth."**

Perhaps she was pursing her lips voluptuously in your direction as your hormones went into involuntary overdrive ... or maybe they were chapped and she was spreading the lip-sil around more evenly.

Perhaps she enjoyed bumping into you in the busy school corridor and was thrilled to raptures of ecstasy when you picked up all her books. Perhaps she regretted sustaining a broken collar-bone as you barged clumsily into her, and perhaps she didn't want your coffee poured all over her newly-finished hand-written essay. Perhaps she likes to be handled roughly ... perhaps not.

That's the problem when you fancy someone ... you read things into the things that you are reading things into. Perhaps ... but perhaps not. In fact, probably not.

How can one tell if one's fancy is fancying one?

One easy solution is to ask the person in question. So:

Gaylord: "Sheila, do you fancy me or am I merely deluding myself and wasting both our time - or mine at least?"

Sheila: "Gaylord, I think you are a fine mathematician but I'm after a theologian ... and anyway you've got a huge nose. I hope that answers your query."

Unfortunately this approach requires vast sums of courage and may not be worth the even greater sums of humiliation and depression that may follow - given a forthright (and negative) reply.

Worse still, she may thump you. Even more humiliating, and, depending on her aim, possibly damaging for life.

In short, when you know you fancy someone take a few days to think about it and work out a plan of action ... but don't take forever.

A few days so that you are sure of your own inclinations towards the subject of your desires, but not a few months because it's a mega-waste of time if they're not remotely interested.

INTERESTING FACT: *According to the law of averages you are likely to fancy someone far more often than the someone you fancy is likely to fancy you.*

After a healthy but shortish wait, try and get into conversation with the subject of your desires (Note: Never the "object" of your desires - as any amateur feminist will happily inform you, we are all people, not objects, certainly not "sex objects".)

Try and do it naturally - controlling your obvious nerves, disguising your sweating and stuttering. Perhaps wear fancy dress, a space suit for example.

An approach such as, "Hey sex-bomb, fancy a night round my place?" will fail with all but a very few girls. (It is also unhelpful in approaching boys.)

As is the approach of too much trepidation: "Er...er...er...Gaythorne...I was wondering if ...er...well, whether..., erm, I don't know how to put this...exactly...but..." (Don't worry about having to put it. Gaythorne wandered off to do something less boring - like watching paint dry - about twenty minutes ago.)

INTERESTING FACT: *Researchers at the University of Illinois found a number of signals showing how a woman tells whether she likes a man or not - without even saying a word. A woman is seen as warm and accepting if she looks into the man's eyes and smiles with an open mouth, makes movements towards him, touches his hand, uses expressive hand gestures while speaking and looking into his wide-open eyes. She is not interested if she frowns, looks around the room or at her fingernails. Brilliant, eh?*

Selecting the Right Person

There are some very simple rules here. If you don't want to move house, you'd better choose someone who lives in the same country. If you are eight foot tall when you're kneeling down, you probably won't be happy with a short person.

Kissing does have a language all of its own but there would be obvious practical problems between a Welsh nationalist who refused to speak English and a West Ham supporter.

Still, knowing who to fall for in the first place could save you a lot of time, money and tissues. Here's our cut-out-and-keep guide.

At School (*a good training ground*)

Good Idea	Bad Idea
Tuck Shop Workers	School Garden Workers
Maths swots	History swots
Head Boys	School Bursar
Head Girls	Caretaker
P E Teachers	Head Teachers

At The Office (*a minefield, best avoided altogether, but if you must...*)

Good Idea	Bad Idea
The Boss	Everyone Else

Nightclub (*a time-honoured tradition thought to be due to alcohol but probably more to do with very poor lighting*)

Good Idea	Bad idea
Anyone who dances worse than you	Anyone who dances first
Bouncers	DJ's
Visible wallet line	Visible panty line
Anyone in stockings	Anyone in white socks
Anyone in black lace	Anyone who does actions to Black Lace

> **Temptation is a woman's weapon and a man's excuse.**
>
> *H. L. Mencken*

STEVE WRIGHT,
Radio One DJ

My first snog was with Janice Ridgeway, aged 7. I remember her, she had long blonde hair and lovely blue eyes. In my primary school dotage I believed she only had eyes for me. We were both exceedingly shy and we kissed very unpassionately in the coal shed. We closed the lid so that we couldn't see what we were doing. The whole thing was most unimpressive.

On the Beach (*difficult to hide what you're really like - relationships beginning here may last about as long as your tan*)

Good Idea	Bad Idea
Lifeguards	Lifeguard groupies
Tide-Fight Organizers	Beach Basketball players
Anyone paler than you	Anyone browner than you
Deckchair attendants	Beach Mission workers
Men in Boxers	Men in pouches or thongs
Beach-hut owners	People who change under a bathrobe

Church (*stuffed full of romantic disasters...and happy families. Ensnarement a certainty. Be warned: in church, they're often looking for the real thing, the complete package, the sound of wedding bells, the marriage made in Heaven*)

Good Idea	Bad Idea
Church Wardens	All Clergy (particularly celibates)
Organists	Choir members
Youth Group Leaders	The man who says *Amen* louder and sooner than anyone else
Ex-Missionaries	Missionaries
Vergers (what do they do anyway?)	Virgins (or them for that matter)
Songs of Praise presenters	TV Evangelists
Thora Hird (Ed: *Really?*)	Harry Secombe

In selecting the right person to fancy, there are basic rules worth considering...unfortunately when you fancy someone, your heart may start beating overtime, the blood rush to your head and fantasy start to rule your waking and sleeping hours. So much for rules.

"ROBBER WHO STOLE A KISS GETS SEVEN YEARS" ran newspaper headlines in 1989, after a man who tried to rob a bank was talked out of it by a young woman who so impressed him that he gave her a kiss.

3

The Chat-Up

Asking Someone Out

Without doubt the most terrifying ordeal any love-lorn lad endures in his lifetime. (Even in these days of sexual equality, it is still usually the lad doing the asking.)

While the custom remains a male prerogative, all the girl can do is sit at home, wash her hair and wait for the phone-call. **(Sixty-nine per cent of all asking out is done on the phone.)**

The knack is for both partners to be friendly, polite and very cool. Do not sound too keen or interested. (It's like buying a house - if you look too keen when you visit, they'll up the asking price.)

> **Lord, I wonder what fool it was that first invented kissing!**
> *Jonathon Swift*

What to say: approaches you might like to consider

The Nonchalant Technique

"Hello Jill...it is Jill isn't it...er...well Enid then...look Enid, I'm going to see the new Charles Bronson film tonight - my favourite actor. I'm going anyway and if it's anything like it was last week there's at least 900 other seats in that Odeon....don't feel pressured or anything...but...er...you'd be welcome to sit in one of them…if you fancy…you know like…er…come along with me…but I'm easy…it's no big deal…er…I'm going anyway…er…(fades)…"

The Forceful Tactic

"Phoebe, I'm buying a Chinese Take-Away for two tonight and you're one of the two…got it?"

The Coy Approach

"Look, I'm a little embarrassed about how to put this, Jemima, but…(five minutes of blushing follows)…oh, don't worry, it was nothing anyway…(runs off pathetically)."

The Desperate Offer

"Look, Belinda, please would you come to church with me tonight, there's a space in my pew, you must come, I need you there with me, please come, do come, I beg you to say 'Yes'…I'm begging you (may need to weep at this point, if Belinda is still within earshot)…I plead with you, I urge you…(If it hasn't worked by now try this optional extra line)…and, by the way, you see this Colt 45, well I'll blow my brains out if you say 'No'."

> There is one thing I would break up over and that is if she caught me with another woman. I won't stand for that.
> **Steve Martin**

The Romantic Approach

"My darling rosebud Heidi, my sweetness and light, my breath of fresh air in a smoke-filled room, the apple of my pie, my soppy valentine message, my sweetest dream of all…er…fancy a curry tonight?"

AUTHORS' GUARANTEE: - THE FOLLOWING CHAT-UP LINES HAVE ALWAYS WORKED FOR US. IF THEY DO NOT WORK FOR YOU, YOU ARE ENTITLED TO ASK FOR YOUR MONEY BACK FROM THE SHOP WHERE YOU PURCHASED THIS BOOK. (The shop are entitled to refuse you and they probably will.)

"Here's a thousand pounds, will you come to McDonalds with me tonight?"

"Here's a thousand pounds, it's only a downpayment - will you come to McDonalds with me tonight? There'll be another thousand when you turn up."

"I've got two seats on the inaugural flight to the moon…interested?"

"Bruce Springsteen and Madonna are coming round for supper tonight, I wondered it you wanted to make up the foursome."

The Use of Roses

Presenting roses to someone when you want to ask them out could well be regarded as a little premature...even a sign of terminal pratishness. No one likes a smarmy twit. But it has been known to work for some.

Specialist Chat-Up Lines

Sometimes the key to securing that all-important first date needs research - especially with fanatics, enthusiasts and specialists of all kinds. Here are some suggestions for using with your prospective date if she is a fanatic of some kind, in politics, sport, music or the like.

Political

"Would you be interested in my gaining control of your means of production...?"(Marxist)

"Do you prefer a hard or soft ECU?"(European)

"Fancy some gilt-edged bonding?"(Capitalist)

"My place...or my other place?"(Tory)

"Have you seen my swing to the left/right?" (general political, delete as appropriate)

"Let's form an alliance...and after a while we'll become one...and then split up again." (Liberal Democrat)

"We've got to stay together, we'd be useless apart." (Unionist)

"Fancy liberating the cows from the town market tonight?" (Free Market Forces)

> **What of soul was left I wonder, when the kissing had to stop.**
> **Browning**

"Of course, I'm a personal friend of Screaming Lord Sutch you know, we're with the same doctor..." (Monster Raving Loony)

"Would you be interested in coming round to test my environmentally friendly washing up liquid?"(Green)

"Of course, with a Tory government no wonder the country's in such a mess...fancy a day-trip to the TUC Conference?"(Labour)

Christian

"I hear there's going to be a love-offering tonight."

"Just looking at you makes me feel all ecumenical."

"Before tonight, I never believed in predestination..."

"I'm pretty flexible. I don't believe a woman should be submissive on the first date."

"You know, I'm really into relationship evangelism."

"You have the body of Amy Grant and the soul of Mother Teresa" (*don't get this confused*).

"What do you think Paul meant when he said, 'Greet everyone with a holy kiss?'"

"I don't see it myself, but people tell me I look like a young Billy Graham."

"Did I tell you that my great-uncle was a personal friend of C.S.Lewis?"

"I just don't feel called to celibacy."

(Thanks to *The Wittenberg Door* magazine.)

Religious Cover-All

"The Lord has revealed to me in a moment of revelation that from before the beginning of time he ordained our meeting here at St Dick's and would like us to get married as soon as possible. As a first step, how about coming to choir practice with me on Thursday?"

Sporting

"I'm sure we share the same goals...and I haven't scored all season"

"Show me your centre-spot..."

"How do you fancy a two-man line-out/scrum/early-bath?"

"I've some experience in bowling maidens over..."

"Middle and leg please..."

"I've never had a hole in one..."

"Let's go the distance..."

Music

"You're certainly in my top ten..."

> **When Elizabeth Siddal died, the poet Dante Gabriel Rossetti said he would never write again, and buried all his unpublished verse in her coffin, only to dig her up seven years later to recover and publish them.**

"You really make my notes quaver..."

"Shall we try for a new entry..."

"I'm fed up with being a single..."

"Fancy a spin in my allegro..."

"Compose yourself...I think we could make sweet music"

"Time for our first movement, my sweet...?"

Feminist

"Of course, I've always felt a man's place was doing the dishes..."

"Could I take you out for a meal?...er...you're paying of course."

"If it wasn't wholly ideologically unacceptable to me, I'd say I could see you on page 3 of *The Sun* anyday..."

"May I say, Alison, that never once have I thought of you as a sex object...fancy an evening discussing male chauvinism?"

"Look, I know that I'm a man but could you forget that for an evening and treat my invitation to attend the woman's writing class as that of another human being."

Arty-Farty

"Would you like to see my etchings?"

"Rodin's 'The Kiss' is such an evocative piece, don't you think?"

"Fancy a visit to The Nude in Art this evening?"

"I couldn't help thinking of you during those love-scenes at the cinema last night..."

"Of course, Luciano and Placido have long been good friends of mine..."

"Oh, you moved, for a second I thought you were a magnificent oil painting..."

Ways of declining an offer to "go out"

You may be on the receiving end of an offer to "walk out" such as the ones used above, and they may not quite work their genius on you...you may have to decline. The traditional form of declining the romantic invitation, often used by the wife to the husband, is, "No, I'm sorry, I'm washing my hair tonight..."

But there are alternatives that our research indicates have a greater ring of authenticity to them. The use of the traditional decline can be insensitive. She may jump to the conclusion that you were just making it up, because, in reality, you wouldn't be seen dead with him on a dark night in the Outer Hebrides.

The following subtle declines are all market-tested and highly successful in the right environment.

"Oh, I am sorry, I'm hamster-sitting tonight"

"Sorry (*floods of tears*) my grandmother's died..." (*No need to tell them it was five years ago*.)

Assume funny voice -"Sorry, wrong number."

"Oh you want Jane Williamssssss... ah...yes...this is Jane William. Wrong number. Goodbye."

"I'd love to but...I'm up to my eyes in embalming fluid"

"I'm dreadfuly sorry but I'm afraid I'm revising for my 11-plus retakes (*or*: cycling proficiency/cookery exam/accountancy finals/etc)."

"I'd love to but my boyfriend might not love me to - or you to. In fact he'd probably kill you."

If the above ripostes prove initially unsuccessful and the pursuant remains in pursuit...the unsubtle approach may be called for. We find the following usually gets the message through reasonably quickly.

"I wouldn't go out with you if you were the last person on earth, I can't stand you, don't ever talk to me again. Now look at what you've done, you've got me in a huff..."

What's in a Kiss

When a rogue kisses you, count your teeth.

Hebrew proverb

The history and science of Kissing

It's a bit odd really, when you come to think about it. The one bit of our bodies into which we spend large amounts of time every day of our waking lives shoving in everything from cod and chips to Cadbury's creme eggs, from steaming smelly curries to the finest caviare, is also the bit we plant on our loved one as a sign of true affection.

Even if she's been eating garlic bread and you're reeking of Prawn Madras, that moment when your lips meet can still create an electric tingle of intimacy that renders your nostrils senseless.

> **The kiss originated when the first male reptile licked the first female reptile, implying in a subtle, complimentary way that she was as succulent as the small reptile he had for dinner the night before.**
>
> *F. Scott Fitzgerald*

Animals are not big snoggers generally, although they've got their own cheeky little romantic numbers - the male house mouse licks the female's mouth, sealions rub mouths, elephants have been known to tip their trunks into the lips of a randy friend, birds knock bills and cats rub noses.

Old as the Bible

And for people too, kissing is as old as kissers, it's been around since the beginning. The Bible even talks of God kissing life into the first people, breathing on man and woman back in the Garden of Eden. After that they took the hint and carried on with the example He had set.

Kissing under the mistletoe dates back to an old Scandinavian myth. After Baldur, god of light, was slain with a dart of mistletoe, his mum, Frigga, goddess of love, decreed that mistletoe should never be used as a weapon, and promised to kiss anyone who passed under it.

Kisses at the end of a letter originated in the Middle Ages when the illiterate signed "X" instead of their name and then kissed the paper to show sincerity.

Mouth to mouth kissing is strong in the Jewish and Christian traditions, and although

> **Let him kiss me with the kisses of his mouth, for thy love is better than wine.**
> *Song of Solomon 1:1, The Bible*

it is unclear whether the Ancient Greeks and Egyptians kissed socially, the Ancient Romans got into some serious snogging.

They even had distinctive words indicating which kind of people were being kissed.

The Romans brought kissing to Britain. But although the British didn't have a word for the practice at that point, it hadn't stopped them doing it anyway - and gradually cultural rules grew up around the practice. Who could kiss whom, when and where and so on.

Mouth To Mouth

For example, mouth to mouth kissing only went on between people who were social equals. Slaves had to do with kissing the boss's sandal, lowly clerics could get as far as the hand of a cardinal or a pope - these days the Pope kisses pilgrims on the head to bless them, or the ground of a new country after his plane has landed. In the Middle Ages, plagued with disease and illness, the bride and groom's kiss at the end of their wedding had legal significance. If one died before the kiss all the wedding gifts had to be returned. Kissing thrived so much that Henry VIII invented a Kissing Comfit breath freshener from the roots of Sea Holly - no monarch had more snogging experience than he did.

No Sabbath Kissing

But it wasn't always as popular as it is today, where couples sometimes snog so blatantly in public places that it might as well be street theatre. (Teenagers are particularly keen to undertake marathon snogging sessions on escalators, in shops or at the seat opposite you in the Wimpy bar - apparently this is for the same reason that a baby discovers the outside world first with its mouth. When teenagers first get into some serious snogging, they are also on a voyage of discovery and want to make the best of the trip.)

Cromwell and his Puritan leadership deemed it a crime to kiss even your wife or husband on the Sabbath. (No wonder Sundays developed such a boring reputation.)

While after the Bolshevik Revolution in Russia in 1917, some local communist party officials declared that kissing was decadent and tried to ban it. Later Mussolini in Italy followed this example, banning any public kissing by men and women.

The Hollywood Snog - Short

Hollywood also played its part in confusing the signals about snogging - even though its very first film was entitled *The Kiss* and lasted thirty seconds back in 1896. But by the 1930s certain codes of acceptable behaviour

> **The longest-ever screen kiss is 185 seconds - it was performed by Ronald Reagan's first wife Jane Wyman lip-sucking Regis Toomey in *You're In The Army Now* made in 1941.**

in the making of films had outlawed "excessive and lustful embraces". A kiss of more than five seconds could land the producer in trouble.

But these were exceptions in a trend towards more and more and more snogging as the years passed - and more and more experimentation with the old lips. Like the arrival of the Love Bite in the fifties, originally a sign of your partner's bloodsuckingly passionate love that you showed your closest friends to impress.

Eventually Hollywood got in on the act big-time - in *The Thomas Crown Affair* made in 1968, Steve McQueen and Faye Dunaway shared the longest screen kiss. Only fifty-five seconds (not as long as the ones witnessed on the back seat of the coach on the school history outing) but it took all day to shoot.

Even though kissing is a mass-market industry today, it still retains a certain mystical ingredient of intimacy and knowledge that other sexual activities cannot match.

Shrinks on Kissing

Psychiatrists point out that while husbands and wives may be unfaithful to each other, they may still carry on an active sexual life with their marriage partner - but it is less likely that they will be kissing their own partner passionately.

There's something about the kiss that gives away too much perhaps. If the infidelity comes to light, the affair ends and the offended party forgives the partner, then the kissing may begin again. The kiss and make-up.

Global Snogging

But even though in some countries today a good snog has never been so popular, not everyone agrees. When Prince Charles and Princess Diana kissed in public during a visit to Oman, something of a diplomatic incident erupted. Omani TV censored pictures of the royal smacker - it might have given their viewers ideas perhaps.

The Japanese would not have been surprised at this approach - they aren't so keen on displays of public passion of the romantic variety. A traditional seductive lip-clincher in Japan is administered not to the mouth but to the nape of the neck. The Chinese meanwhile are said to tickle each other's feet as a preliminary to love-making and don't even have a word for "kiss". Malays, Aboriginals and Somalis aren't big kissers - the Eskimos and Papuans rub noses. A Polynesian alternative to the kiss is called the *mitakuku* and involves tugging hairs out of your beloved's eyebrows with your teeth. Ouch! (*For more detail on cross-cultural kissing see "Snogging All Over The World" at the back of this book.*)

Going Weak at the Knees - The Scientific Explanation

The last thing you think about in the middle of a serious clincher is what exactly are the chemical reactions being caused in and around you - and your partner's - bio-system. But judging by the funny movements in other parts of a man's body and the propensity of women to faint (in a good Hollywood snog anyway) kissing gets the body going like few other things, excepting, perhaps, a sudden dose of electric current. Not so different in fact.

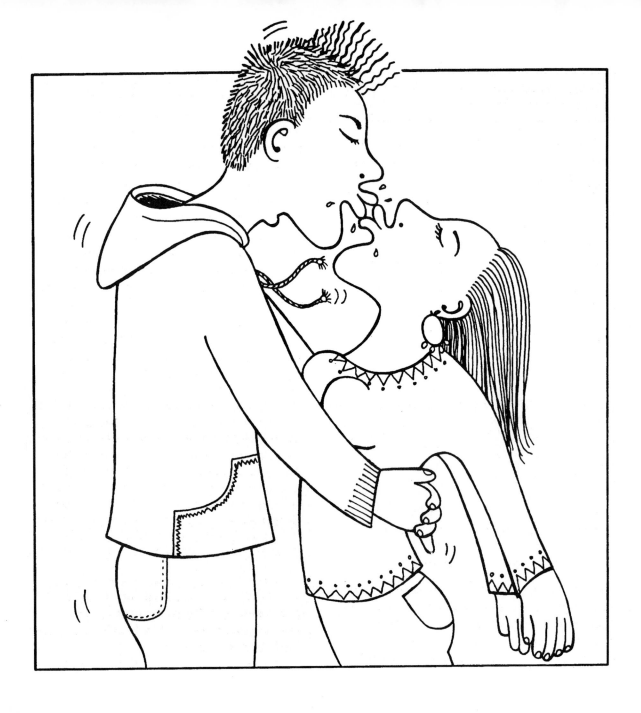

After just seven snogging seconds (true, time sometimes changes meaning mid-snog) the body starts to work chemical wonders.

Both boys and girls have developed things called sebaceous glands from puberty onwards which are around the lips and inside the mouth. Stick another pair of lips on your own and the pressure acts like a trigger firing off this sebum liquid. A sexual trigger in fact, dictating whether we appreciate - or deprecate - our snogpiece depending on their personal taste and smell.

Sebum-Firing

A decent sebum-firing smacker bumps up the heartbeat from the usual 72 beats a minute to 95, raising the pulse rate and sending blood tearing round the body like a greyhound out of its trap. All of which makes you feel warmer, even as if you are glowing a little, and the lips become engorged, softening and swelling, turning a deeper than normal red.

Hence the popularity of red lipstick.

The Lips Have it - Do they?

An American study in the 1950s investigated how a group of women, sometimes wearing lipstick, sometimes not, were seen and assessed by male job interviewers.

Lipsticked women were always judged more talkative, more outgoing and more frivolous than their bare-mouthed sisters. And a clear indication that lips - or at least lipstick - could mislead a man in his judgement of sexuality lay in the fact that the men remembered the skirts of lipsticked women as being shorter than they really were.

Whether the size of your lips is important or not, if you are a woman, some women clearly believe that bigger is best - at the end of the 1980s a new trend emerged from the West Coast of America in which women began putting their money where their mouths were, literally. They started buying themselves Zyoderm pouts...having plastic surgeons inject them with copious amounts of a substance

> **Dr Michael O'Connor of the Coronary Prevention Group, told *Today* newspaper that someone suffering from heart disease could have an attack brought on by the excitement of kissing. The newspaper reported that every time couples get into a clinch, pulse rates soar, putting hearts under pressure. "It is possible that the stress and tension of kissing could be bad for you", said the Doctor. "Anything that causes excitement makes your blood flow quicker."**
>
> **But in the final analysis he thought the risks were outweighed by the potential benefits of a good snog. "On the whole affairs of the heart go better with a little kissing."**

CARON KEATING,
TV Presenter

His name was Colin Manavna and we were both ten years old. We were the stars of the school play, *The Frog and the Princess*. He was the frog and I was the princess. After our last night there was a party and I distinctly remember that I kissed him non-stop all night. In fact we kissed so much my lips were rather swollen, they looked like boiled worms. I think it put him off as we never kissed again.

and helping decide whether they pursue the love-making or not.

But the most powerful reason of all for why we kiss, whether we are conscious of it or not, has to be what a kiss says - to the kissers and to the watchers. A kiss has a powerful symbolic value, signalling the union of two bodies into one body, joined at an open mouth, sharing the breath of their lives with each other. Romantic, huh?

called Zyoplast which fattens their lips and leaves no trace. But it's not cheap and it doesn't last that long - especially if you're a serious kisser. The more you snog, the quicker your Zyoplasted lips will deflate to normal size.

But why do we kiss?

Well there's no question that it has a lot to do with the food exchanged between mother and baby in ancient cultures - not so much a bite to eat as a kiss to eat.

When two lovers kiss they rediscover that special intimate security in the bond between mother and child. Then there's the chemical business - telling each partner about the other,

A man in York was ordered by a judge to pay £50 to a young woman for "insulting behaviour". The man admitted in court that walking down the street one day, he was so excited by the sight of the young woman that he dashed over the road and tried to plant a smacker on her.

4
So They Said No

Survey after survey has pointed out that 90% of the people asked out by 90% of us, er, ... said no ... er ... 90% of the time.

So now it's happened to you as well. Don't worry. You are not alone - it's happened to everyone. Remember, there are other birds in the air, other pies in the oven, other ... er ... clichés in this book. Perhaps they were too embarrassed to accept your marvellous offer of a night at "The Eagle and Arms", perhaps

> **The sound of a kiss is not as loud as that of a cannon but its echo lasts longer.**
>
> **O. W. Holmes**

they'd already talked to your last partner and believed the stories about you dribbling during the simplest meal - perhaps they had taken a vow of celibacy which, in order to preserve its secret nature, they had been forced to cover up with an insensitive lie in relation to the colour of your teeth.

Or perhaps they simply didn't like the look of you. The fact of the matter is that most people judge other people most of the time, on the basis of the flimsiest of evidence - glass eye,

> **Only time can heal your broken heart, just as only time can heal his broken arms and legs.**
>
> **Miss Piggy**

> **Then she kissed me and I knew it was puppy love. Her nose was cold.**

wooden leg, constant attendance of a psychiatric nurse etc.

Coping with Rejection

Here are some ideas for coping with that dull, aching pain that accompanies rejection - that feeling, completely false though it is, that you are worthless, no, worse than worthless. Worthevenless. Worthevenlessthanworthless. (*Yes, thank you.* Ed.)

Reading

This can be done by taking out a book and reading it. If the story line is good or the pictures interesting, it can take your mind off the silly old cow who turned you down. (*What a plonker.*)

Watching Telly

Again, a simple enough idea but, if *Neighbours* is on, it can easily remind you that your life isn't that bad really. At least you don't have to learn lines like that.

Television watching can often help you divert your mental interest from the old bat who declined your attractive invitation to an evening's ten-pin bowling. Unfortunately television watching has its own health hazards, such as the slow death of the brain.

Eating

Particularly useful if you'd already booked a meal for two in anticipation that she'd accept. Now you can eat hers too. Serve her right, silly old twit. (*Bet she smells anyway.*)

Visiting Interesting Places

Again, can take the mind off the trouble at hand. Best to avoid going near her street. (*Wouldn't want to anyway. Probably got B.O., like her.*)

The Vow of Celibacy

More complicated approach and rather more final, but celibacy has often been considered by depressed suitors in the first flush of rejection.

On the whole though - celibacy being a good thing if you're cut out for it - it's better given than taken in spite.

The main merit of The Vow of Celibacy is that once people know you have taken it, you don't always get the impression that they are thinking, "Aaaah, isn't it sad...he'd make someone a lovely husband..." Now they know you're not in the market...so they can mind their own business.

> **Love is not the dying moan of a distant violin - it is the triumphant twang of a bedspring.**
> **S. J. Perelman**

The Gentle Art of Social Kissing

Unromantic Snogging

Not all kissing is of a romantic nature of course – when your granny kisses you goodnight, when a footballer slurps another after a goal, when the pope lip-butts the tarmac of another country – the kissing is of a different order to that involved between the fancier and the fancied, the lover and the loved.

But there is some confusion about just when social kissing is appropriate and when it is not. British men, for example, are uneasy at the European tendency (see below) to kiss each other on the cheek or even the lips on significant occasions.

It may be fine on the football field – although not on the cricket field – but for one man to kiss another in public in British society will almost certainly see them labelled as something other than heterosexual in orientation. (This itself is deemed unsavoury in some sectors of modern society).

Uneasy Kissing

Some argue that the British man's uneasiness at public kissing may stem from unsettling childhood experiences with Aunt Gertrude, slobbering all over him with her granite lips -

and in front of all his sisters too. Research here is inconclusive. It's probably got something to do with British reserve as well. Arabs or Russian soldiers might walk round hand in hand, but in the UK at least, we certainly don't kiss our same-sex friends like the Victorians did.

INTERESTING FACT: *An experiment was conducted at an American University where a couple of girls went round arm-in-arm like nineteenth-century bosom*

The Marylebone Cricket Club (MCC), the leading cricket authority, issued a strict new ruling to players at the start of the 1991 season - no more kissing. This came after fears that England's cricketers were beginning to imitate the antics of their footballing colleagues who lavish each other with sloppy smackers every time the ball goes in the back of the net. Lt Colonel John Stephenson, MCC Secretary, said, "Too many cricketers are behaving like professional footballers - it's a disgrace. I don't see why they can't just shake hands like they did in the old days after getting a wicket. It sets a poor example for younger players."

friends, with the result that everyone assumed they were lesbian lovers.

The confusion can make for extreme difficulty in the social calendar - for example, on your arrival at a friend's house for a dinner party, does your hostess expect you to smack her cheek with your full lips...or is she expecting you to shake her hand?

The Use of the Hands in Social Kissing

Men at least can choose an alternative to kissing women on the cheek. A kiss on the hand has come to signal old-fashioned, romantic values such as chivalry and gallantry. Today it would probably suggest you are a bit of a plonker.

INTERESTING FACT: *There are dangers in too much social kissing. According to one recent report, it can lead to head lice, passed on when you touch heads. The medical journal* The Lancet *even claimed that kissing a bride at a wedding can be unhealthy - you might catch germs from someone who had earlier kissed her.*

The European Dimension

With the arrival of the Single European Market, the population of the British Isles will have to adjust to an entirely new cultural approach to the Kiss.

Already there is some confusion in the country. The Rev. R. J. Kingsbury, concerned to see things done properly, wrote to *The Times* complaining, "I have to kiss rather a lot of people over the Christmas period. I gather one makes a noise at the moment of impact. Last year the prevailing sound at the church door was 'Mwa!' Is this still de rigueur or is there a new exhalation of which I should be aware?"

The Cheek of It

An organisation calling itself the European Democratic Union has been looking into the differences in social custom in Europe, including the use of the lips. The French, it says, kiss on both cheeks while the Belgians insist on a third kiss - not necessarily on a different cheek. Some say that it doesn't matter which cheek is offered first. But *Business Life*, the magazine of British Airways, claims that Britons start with the right cheek, while the French and Belgians start with the left.

The Germans like a formal little bow over an outstretched hand, while the Spanish have a two-tier system of formal and informal. But if the Germans go in for a great deal of vigorous handshaking, in places like Poland, Austria and Hungary handkissing is still very common.

According to the European Democratic Union, although French politicians do drop ceremonial kisses on each other, apart from that male, kissing is restricted to close family relations.

Sexy English Reserve

Businesswomen in Europe don't have to kiss each other either, unless they really want to - which is okay too. Woman are bigger kissers of each other on the Continent but it's not a big deal. Nor is it compulsory.

Although the English are known for a traditional reserve in the area of meeting and greeting, this approach has its fans outside the British Isles.

"Give me the English anytime", said the actress Zsa Zsa Gabor. "I hope Englishmen don't adopt continental customs. It is quite nice when men kiss a lady's hand but I just adore the reserve of Englishmen. They are rough, tough, sexy and exciting. The French and Italians are always kissing hands but they are full of bull. The Germans are quite like the English but they have less humour."

According to Harold Brooks-Baker who is writing a book on European etiquette, kissing trends are changing in the UK.

"Up until the mid-19th century, kissing on both cheeks was usual among the upper classes. Now it is enjoying a revival in the middle classes.

"As a foreigner, if you make a mistake it can always be blamed on the country you come from."

The Time and The Place

Any time of day or night is okay for social kissing as long as you do it before you've got into conversation with the person - you do it as a greeting, you don't break off a sentence to suddenly plant a smacker on them. Or, if you are leaving somewhere, you do it as you leave...if you get caught up in more goodbye chat, you'll have to do the smacking again.

Don't do it at work - it's bad for working relationships - and don't do it on the lips. Lips have to do with passion, and the social kiss has nothing to do with passion. If it does it's probably more than social kissing the person is after.

Types of Social Kissing

Kissing a superior - like the Queen - you'll find that just as you are about to touch bodies, the Queen will turn her face away from you, leaving her right royal cheek for you to land on. Actually this Right Royal Cheek is more a touch-down than a landing. Oh, and don't upset her make-up.

Another kiss of the social variety is The *Puffer* - used for people who are new acquaintances. They lean necks towards each other, line up their heads and cheeks about half a foot apart, and make a soundless puffing action into thin air, puckering the lips appropriately.

Like this one, but combined with a sharp, strangulated growling noise, is a kiss practised by the socially pretentious. If it is performed by members of the acting fraternity they'll probably follow it with a ridiculous stuck-up noise that sounds like "Darling, how simply lovely to see you...".

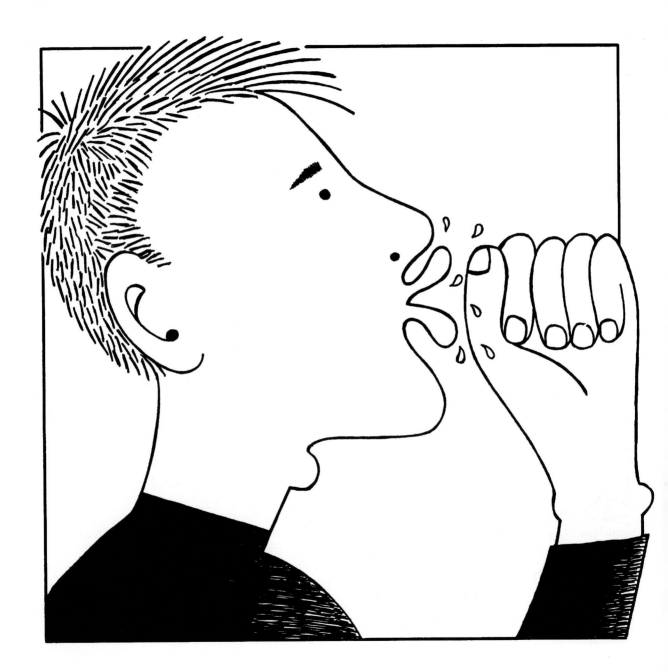

5
So They Said Yes

Getting Started as a Snogger

So, you have a date and, most importantly, because this is what the whole of this book is about, you may get the chance to do some snogging.

You will need to get in some practice at home first: but as is the nature of these things and however well you get on with your parents, boys will not be able to practise with their mothers, girls will not be able to practise with their fathers. (*After all, if you*

> **A kiss that speaks volumes is seldom a first edition.**
>
> *Clare Whiting*

did, they might catch on that you might be practising for a date, and half the fun of a date is that they don't catch on. They might want to come along for a start. Or, worse still, they might want to give you advice - "Well, son, in my day, there was no kissing the young lady until we'd been safely married for five years...so don't be too precipitate.")

Snogging Yourself

A useful place to start is with yourself.

1. Take your right hand and raise it to within six inches of your lips.

2. Now, without letting go of your hand, take your lips and purse them, keeping them in

PHILIP SCHOFIELD,
TV Presenter

Why is it that all first kisses seem to take place behind the bike sheds? Mine certainly did, at school in Cornwall. I'd better not mention her name as she'd be exceedingly embarrassed and is probably married with many children. It was just a very boring, dull, plain peck on the cheek - definitely no tongues. The relationship lasted five seconds.

constant touch with each other for the moment.

3. Close your eyes and imagine Blodwen in all her glorious beauty standing in front of you

4. Now, bring your right hand in towards your pursed lips (we know it's exciting but don't unpurse them yet, please) and make contact, gently but firmly.

5. You don't want to frighten your hand so don't make any sudden moves. Gradually, keeping your eyes closed and your imagination on at full throttle, unpurse your lips. (The firm but tender crush of skin on skin sends a violent thrill down your spine, you are carried away in raptures, you are in dream world, strange apparently unrelated parts of your body are moving

mysteriously...you are getting carried away...just like us.)

6. If you've got a cold and your nose is blocked you may find that you have expired because you couldn't breathe. Pick yourself up and start again.

7. Suck your hand, creating kissy-kissy sounds. Get that out of your system because Blodwen will go bonkers if you make kissy-kissy sounds on her golden lips.

8. Keep your tongue to yourself. (There are plenty of pages in this book yet - your tongue's time will come.)

9. Draw your lips together again and...relax...and...release...and stop.

(10. If that's your mother standing by the door looking bewildered, tell her that as you left home ten years ago and she's a guest in your house, it's up to you how you choose to, um, er...untangle irritating hairs on the back of you hand.)

Practise in the Home

Using a friendly mirror can be useful to perfecting one's snogging technique.

> **In 1909 a group of American men called the Anti-Kissing League formed, pledging never to kiss their wives again because it was unhealthy.**

> **We only deliberately waste time with those we love, it is the purest sign that we love someone if we choose to spend time idly in their presence when we could be doing something more constructive.**
>
> ***Sheila Cassidy***

> **Love is like photographic film. It has to be developed in the dark.**

Unfortunately mirrors can be a bit on the cold side and will not be able to reciprocate your heady emotions. Can also give way to vanity...kissing your own image.

Another drawback is the risk involved - it can be fatally humiliating if your mother bursts into the room while you're lip-smacking your wardrobe.

Practising Snogging Someone Else

Can have practical difficulties - almost certainly no one will want to snog you. The kind of person who would agree, you may not want to practise on. For example the dog.

Practising on a Relative

Similar to above and can be a bit of a give-away - they may see through your elaborate explanation about researching your biology homework and guess that you're practising

> **One American anthropologist claimed that 37% of men keep their eyes closed when kissing but 97% of women do.**

for your first date. Disastrous if, for example, the price of your grandmother's confidentiality is that she has to come with you.

Practical Preparation

Blow your nose, spike your spots, wash all over, put some deodorant under your armpits, wear a clean shirt, cut your nails, clip your nasal hair, gargle...all the usual. Are we sounding like your mother?

Dress

Yes, essential.

Underwear

Yes, again. (*Note:Surveys suggest that women change their undies every day but men change them now and again. Mostly again.*)

6
Your First Date

Dating is a fifties expression which seems a little old-fashioned to the modern ear - but we like it so we're sticking with it.

You might prefer phrases such as "courting" (even more old-fashioned), "walking out" (confusingly, this can also be done with a dog), "going out" (can also be ambiguous, might be taken merely as leaving the room for example) or "itemising" as in the expression, "Are they an item?" (*This last is a little unromantic*)

> **"Who was that man I saw you kissing last night?"**
> **"What time was it?"**

> **Love is like war, easy to begin but very hard to stop.**
> **H. L. Mencken**

a) Where to Take Them.

Cinema

The classic venue for a first date, basically because it's dark and you don't have to look at each other's embarrassed faces.

Tradition states that it doesn't matter what the film is as your new partner is doubtless more attractive/brainy/sexy/successful/than Kelly McGillis/Arnold Schwarzenneger/Kim Basinger/Micky Mouse.

That's tradition for you.

In the authors' experience this is usually only true in the dark and with your eyes squinting so much you look like a teddy bear in a jumble sale.

Choice of film is crucial and will reveal a lot about the kind of person you are and perhaps what you want your new partner to be.

Film	About Him	About Her
Gone With The Wind	Egomaniac who says "Damn" when excited	Stupid and emotional
Amadeus	Wild, talented, and likely to die early	Daft, sleepy and likely to die early
The Fly	Forget it	Scientific, starry-eyed and off child birth
La Pomme De La Fenetre Choisisi Le Terrain des portes	Linguist and Show-off	French
Rambo	Delusions of power	Delusions about you
Batman	Likes wearing tights	Likes men in tights
Jesus	Wants to convert you	Wants to convert you

So be careful. It may be best to avoid any film that needs concentration, has a good script or good acting and features anything resembling a plot. Any Richard Gere film would be fine.

The Restaurant

This illustrates definite keenness on your behalf. Is this a good idea, bearing in mind that you'll have to look at each other? If you do have any tendency toward dribbling, it's hard to disguise it in such a public place. It is just possible you may be able to book a table with "restricted view" - perhaps situated around a pillar so that your partner can't actually see the gravy pouring down your chin onto your shirt. (*Warning: a restaurant is not advised for chronic dribblers.*)

In fact be careful whatever kind of eaterie you go for, some foods can embarrass as you eat, others can embarrass later. Always offer to pay for your meal. Forget this simple rule and you'll end up in prison.

> **"Girls run after my kisses."**
> **"So what, after mine they are limp."**

Going for a Drink

Should be cheap and cheerful, a good casual start. Points to remember;

1. Inebriation is not attractive. It's difficult to continue a romance if your partner is familiar with your breakfast. It's difficult to feel any romantic feelings towards someone continually slipping off the pavement into the gutter.

2. Cheese and Onion crisps are great but leave you smelling like a Franco-Dutch gastronomic disaster. Not a kissing incentive.

3. You might meet your friends - or worse, your date's friends.

4. If there is a drunk present on the evening, he will undoubtedly come and sit next to you.

5. Drinking leads invariably to burping and this could be catastrophic if planning a quick good-night encounter later on.

Going for a Walk

A much under-used and under-valued idea. Undoubtedly the cheapest option available. And a definite opportunity to show off your conversation and conservation skills. Can sometimes lead to a roll in the hay - even if it's only a ham roll.

b) Where Not To Take Them

Lovers' Lane

Oh dearie me, no. Merely suggests you are a randy devil, not a romantic fool. Anyway it'll probably be full and what if your partner has clearly been there before? Dare you take this risk? How far did s/he go then?...the questions are endless and could fatally damage your relationship before you have even reached pecking stage.

Swimming Baths

You are in effect showing all your wares at once - where else would you stand in front of your new partner in just a few inches of cloth. *High humiliation-potential.*
  Although the Bible enjoins us not to judge by appearances, most people tend to all the same, and you'll only encourage them if you're wearing that ridiculous thong.

Remember:

1. your costume will be too tatty/small/unfashionable/tight

2. your partner will dive/swim/jump much better than you

3. you have to walk through that horrible anti-verruca pool

You'll emerge from your swim, hair standing on end, red-eyed, stinking of chlorine and with that funny red rubber band still attached to your arm. A less attractive figure is hard to imagine.

Church

Most people go to church because they have special reason to - to say thanks to God for life and all its excitements, including kissing.

But beware that if your potential snogger is not on speaking terms with God as yet, you could be jeopardising a potentially beautiful relationship by inviting her along on a Sunday morning if - and only you can judge this - the service is often anaesthetically dull and deadly boring.

A secondary danger to be aware of is that the vicar may spot the "new face", assume they do not "love the Lord" as yet and try and spend the service saving them to your crimson-coloured embarrassment.

Worse, your friends may pounce afterwards, some on you to chastise you for being "unequally yoked" with a non-believer - some on your partner to lead them gently but firmly to the Light in the next five minutes.

A potentially disastrous venue for a date.

On the other hand your partner might admire you for having the courage to take her on such an "alternative" date - no other boyfriend will have been half so imaginative. And she might find everyone so warm and friendly that she's quite taken by the whole experience and wants to show her gratitude from the top to the bottom of her lips.

Last Minute Checklist

Dealing with Nerves - Take a psychiatrist with you or a trained counsellor. Snap out of it. Slap yourself. Douse yourself in cold water.

Dealing with your Mother (if she's come with you.) Give her a fiver and send her to the bingo.

INTERESTING FACT: *According to an American researcher into sexual mores, women can tell things about men by the way they behave on a date. A warm open smile suggests genuine interest; if he licks his lips a lot, it may indicate he is sexually passionate; if he touches you a lot perhaps he is bold, confident and sensual, but don't be fooled if he is eager to compliment you - it may just be using flattery to get ahead.*

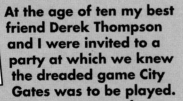

**JAKKI BRAMBLES,
Radio One DJ**

At the age of ten my best friend Derek Thompson and I were invited to a party at which we knew the dreaded game City Gates was to be played. This involved copious amounts of snogging. As we didn't want to look stupid we practised on each other beforehand. To be perfectly honest it was all a bit wet and messy and I went cross-eyed.

44

Valentine's Day

…is celebrated on 14th February but according to a don in the USA who spent eight years researching the subject, we've got it all wrong.

Professor H. Kelly says we are celebrating St Valentine of Rome, martyred on 14th February, when we should be remembering St Valentine of Genoa, who died on 3rd May.

Off His Head in Love

Others say they were one and the same person. The day derives from the unfortunate saint who fell in love with his executioner's blind daughter. He restored her sight by a miracle but on the orders of the Emperor Claudius (who seemed such a nice bloke on the television) he was dragged out onto the streets of Rome in AD 269 and was clubbed to death anyway. Then they cut his head off.

His bad luck didn't end there. He also disappeared from the list of saints when several mythical characters lost their holy status some years ago - 14th February, St Valentine's Day, is now actually the property of two saints, missionary brothers Cyril and Methodius, declared joint patrons of Europe by Pope John Paul II in 1981.

As for the date - in the Middle Ages, people exchanged love tokens on 14th February because it was believed to be the day when birds chose their mates. A custom first mentioned by Chaucer.

In 1827, when postage was paid on delivery, the Post Office received scores of complaints from the recipients of insulting Valentine's cards. The Post Office refunded the

> **A kiss is the shortest distance between two people.**

postage costs of those that were libellous.

The Victorians turned Valentine's Day into an industry and the Victoria and Albert Museum has a vast collection of Valentine Cards from Victorian times, including some highly elaborate hand-made creations.

The first recorded Valentine card - not a letter - was sent by Samuel Pepys, who wrote about it in his diary. But in his day people didn't choose their Valentines, they cast lots for them and were expected to send them a present - usually a pair of gloves.

Unromantic Valentines

But not all Valentine's Day events are connected with love - on 14th February 1929, Al Capone machine-gunned the leaders of Bugsy Moran's gang in Chicago. And it wasn't a message of love and affection that

Muslim leaders sent to Salman Rushdie, author of *The Satanic Verses*, on 14th February 1988 when they issued their *fatwa* - death sentence - on him.

In fact although Valentine's Day may be a day to declare love to another, for many people it can be a sad and depressing occasion, perhaps because they don't have anyone to show love to or don't feel loved by the person they would like to be loved by. A survey carried out in Birmingham showed a 30% rise in the number of teenagers trying to kill themselves on Valentine's Day. Other people can see the humour in it - a New York company devised an ingenious way to off-load unsold blooms. It offered a "Drop Dead" message service, despatching wilted roses tied in black ribbon to the one that got away. In Texas, one TV advertisement urged, "This Valentine's Day, get your lover a plastic surgery voucher."

7

The Second Date

(Same person, next time)

Snogging, it must be said, is a mystic ritual, a sacred activity, not to be undertaken lightly - nor necessarily on the first date. Fools rush in where snoggers fear to tread, while the best snogging careers don't necessarily start as soon as the couple have met.

Let things take their course, let the temperatures rise, let the imagination wander...there's plenty of time. Don't panic.

But if your partner agrees to "go out" on a second date, a follow-up, a return leg, a rematch...it's only fair to assume that they're game for a snog. Or at least a peck.

> **...we did one of those quick awkward kisses where each of you gets a nose in the eye.**
> **Clive James, Unreliable Memoirs**

Trying to get that first kiss

First Aid

Try a subtle trip-up - you'll have to grab her to save her from the fall. If you can't manipulate a lip-graze here, get drastic - Save Her Life. "Accidentally" (heh, heh) push her out into some oncoming traffic - then pull her back in the nick of time, thus saving her life. Surely her gratitude will be lip-led.

The peck

Easy really, just watch some hens. Then, as you are walking down the street, dart your neck out and "peck" her cheek. As your lips return, don't try and bring any food back with you.

The lip-synch

Like miming...pretend you are doing it for fun, then ravish her round the molesters.

The use of the arms

Always useful, particularly if your partner is trying to get away during your first kiss.

The question of physical rejection and personal insult ("*Help, help, Officer, I'm being assaulted....*")

It may be that your partner has no intention of kissing you in a month of Sundays and is entirely unaware of your amorous intentions towards her lips. This may become clear if they begin shouting hysterically and screaming for help - for example from the police - during your first attempted snog. In these circumstances, it is probably best to call it a day and head for home.

> **"I love you terribly."**
> **"You certainly do."**

Being taken by surprise

It may be that just as you think the evening is over, as your heart is sinking at the prospect of telling your mates fibs about "how far you went"...worse still, in fact, at the prospect that perhaps she doesn't fancy you at all...suddenly you are taken by surprise.

The match isn't over until it's over, as a football commentator once said. And sometimes your partner, who has been a little standoffish all evening, warm but not on fire perhaps, may suddenly turn and plant one on you just as you are dropping her off at her home.

And even if she doesn't, console yourself with the thought that perhaps she wanted to ...but didn't want to embarrass you, wasn't sure if you wanted your lips smacked or not.

No first kiss is like the one that takes you by surprise. And if you aren't taken by surprise, well there's always next time.

(*Note: If after 37 dates you still haven't touched lips it may be that you are both too nervous to take the other by surprise or by any other way...now is probably the time to forget all the rules and dive in, lips first.*)

> **"I told you to stop kissing me."**
> **"I did, several times."**

Top Twenty Kissing

If Music Be The Food of Love

If you want to start or end a romance but somehow don't have the guts to do it, getting your favourite DJ to play a song on the radio might be just the ticket.

Radio presenters are a much-maligned group of people who are nice, humble, loving...(*Yes, that's enough. Ed*)
There are plenty of kissing songs to choose from, one for every occasion.

To Get Things Going request any of the following:

Your Kiss is Sweet - Syreeta
Kiss Me With Your Mouth - Stephen "Tin Tin" Duffy
I Want To Kiss You All Over - Exile
Your Kiss Is On My List - Hall and Oates
Kiss - Prince
And Then He Kissed me - The Crystals
or And Then He Kissed Her - The Beach Boys
Kiss The Bride - Elton John

To slow things down or finish it off altogether :

The Last Kiss - David Cassidy
Na Na Hey Hey Kiss Him Goodbye - Steam

(*or to be really certain, ask for Bananarama's version*)
Kissing a Fool - George Michael
Kiss This Thing Goodbye - Del Amitri
You're Dribbling - Sally and Ivor

Songs Never To Be Asked for Whatever the Occasion, However Desperate:

Save Your Kisses for Me - Brotherhood of Man
Sugar Candy Kisses - Matt and Katie Kissoon
Sealed with a Kiss - Jason Donovan
Lucky Lips - Cliff Richard
Suck My Kiss - The Orb

If nothing fits write your own. Don't be overawed by the talents of Gershwin, Lennon and McCartney or Timmy Mallet. Why not compose your own kissing couplet or snog serenade? Not only can it be tailor-made to fit your own individual requirements (essential if dating an Arnold or Agnes), but the chances of impressing your intended are manifold. If Chas and Dave can get away with it so can you.

> **Husbands are like fires – they go out when unattended.**
> *Cher*

GARY DAVIES,
Radio One DJ

I first experienced the joys of kissing when I was down the local youth club in Manchester at the age of 13. Her name was Julia and I had fancied her for ages. It came to that point in the proceedings that is known as "smooch-time". I suddenly got all nervous as I hadn't got the faintest idea what to do. It was a definite closed lip peck and I remember thinking, "Well, what's all the fuss about?"

Here are some useful rhymes to get you going:

Lips: zips, chips, nips, hips and ships.eg.

There was a young woman whose lips
Looked rather like two large ships
When she opened them wide
You could see her fillings inside
Along with some rather old chips

or **Snog**: dog, hog, fog, bog.

A man had just started to snog
A girl, but got lost in the fog
When it started to clear
He said, Let's go for a beer
She said, No let's go the whole hog

Sex is emotion in motion.
Mae West

or **Teeth**: Beith (Alan), Heath (Ted), Reith (Lord), Keith (Sheath)

There once was a woman whose teeth
Had been much acquainted with Ted Heath
She said, C'mon you sucker
Let's go for a pucker
He said, No - it was banned by Lord Reith

Tongue: dung, bung, hung, young,

The way to stay looking young
Is to bathe every day in some dung
You'll feel a lot stronger
You can kiss for longer
And double the length of your tongue

(*As you can see, this kind of romantic verse requires no talent at all.*)

Love is an itch around the heart that you can't scratch.

8
That First Snog In Detail

Keeping Your Teeth out of the Way - (*Slip them in your Pocket*)

The most common mistake with the first kiss is to confuse the person you are kissing with a meal you are eating.

Unfortunately, in the same way that if you plunged your face into a plate of spaghetti and chips you'd get it all over your face, most first-kissers end up getting their partner all over their face.

Take it slowly, calmly, tentatively...

If your partner reels backward mid-snog,

> **The record for the longest kiss ever is seventeen days, ten and a half hours.**

> **He hasn't actually kissed me yet, but he steamed up my glasses a couple of times.**

choking badly and holding on to a nearby wall to stay upright, this probably means you have been too vigorous and you have unintentionally butted their falsies half-way down their throat.

Tip. Don't be too ambitious - keep your teeth to yourself. For the time being you should probably keep your mouth shut too - that electric tingling sensation as lip touches lip should suffice for sensual satisfaction on your first kiss.

Getting the teeth re-pointed later

See a dentist.

Mouth Ulcers

It's not very, er, tasteful to have to mention these in a family book like this but mouth ulcers are a fact of life and a serious kissing-disincentive to your partner. However painful they may be, if you want to keep kissing, you probably shouldn't tell them. (If your ulcers are giving you too much of a problem try calling the Ulcer Volunteer Force - otherwise see their genuine advantages in our companion volume *Advanced Snogging Tricks for Circus Performers*.)

Internal Mouth Bleeding

This can occur if your partner has clumsily knifed your gum with his/her incisors. You may think that on the face of it (sorry) one person's mouth cannot get inside another's to do damage, but the science of kissing has its own internal logic.

According to dental research, kissing cuts down tooth decay. But why do dentists have such bad breath?

Inexperience can result in serious internal damage...but it's always worth the risk and usually worth the damage.

Chapped Lips

This is what you can get when, if you are a girl, your chap is getting a little over-excited during kissing. (See also - Chappess Lips)

Chappess Lips

See above.

Avoiding Facial Blemishes

Tricky this. You don't want to snog their spots but if there's one positioned on their upper or lower lip and you really love them, well, you probably can't avoid it.

Touching spots can be avoided if you kiss through a plastic bag - but your partner will usually notice this and realise that something is wrong. (Then they will become all self-conscious and embarrassed, especially if you

George Romeny and Mary Abbott were married in 1756 but he left her with two children after five years because Sir Joshua Reynolds told him that art and politics didn't mix. He returned to his wife 37 years later, probably mad and empty-pocketed, to be nursed devotedly by her until his death in 1802.

are turning blue.) Not recommended. (Can also utilise houshold washing up-gloves or metal fencing.)

Careful contortion of the lips, weaving with agility around the difficult areas, can be achieved with practice. It is more difficult to do it without your partner noticing.

INTERESTING FACT: *Researchers (what a great piece of research!) have found that a lot of information can be gleaned on your partner simply from your first kiss.*

Elayne Kahn, for example. A Director of a Sex and Marriage centre in New York, argues that if the man keeps his eyes open during the snog, he may be guarded, cautious and reticent about expressing emotions - perhaps someone who seeks to control the relationship.

If he is a hard kisser, he may have no other kiss in his repertoir and could be trying to hide his own vulnerability. The girl should be wary of the boy who is so eager to dominate that he literally shoves his tongue down your throat. Also a man who kisses repeatedly in public perhaps feels the need to advertise his sexuality to others - he may be plagued by doubts about how sexy he really is. While what she calls the "everybody kisser", the man kissing anyone and everyone in sight, may be genuinely open to intimate human contact and eager for love - not the complete wally he appears to be!

Phrase by Phrase Kissing

Kissing of course - or snogging as we are calling it in this book - has its own special underground language, such as, er, "snogging". This curious lingo is understood often only by aficionados and professional snogsters or kissomaniacs. As your snogging abilities develop and new opportunities present themselves - attached no doubt to the faces of new partners - you may need to learn what your partner is trying to say to you in this special coded language of the kiss. This phrase-by-phrase guide could come in useful - just pull it out mid-snog when you think there's more to what's being said than meets your ear.

"Any chance of a quick peck?"
Meaning: *Let's snog.*

"Shall we kiss?"
Meaning: *Yes, we shall.*

"I'm not going any further than kissing."
Meaning: *Of course, I don't mind where you kiss me!*

"Do you french-kiss?"
Meaning: *You're just about to.*

"How do you find my kissing?"
Meaning: *Pretty good aren't I ?!*

"Could we kiss softly tonight?"
Meaning: *Last night you couldn't have done more damage if you'd used scissors.*

"That was the greatest kiss of my life."
Meaning: *That was the greatest kiss all evening.*

"Er, let's not be too hasty."
Meaning: *Keep your tongue to yourself.*

"You're quite a romantic aren't you?"
Meaning: *You don't have to kneel and kiss my hand every time you come around.*

"I'm still quite shy about kissing in many ways - it's a very personal thing after all."
Meaning: *We may be getting married tomorrow but I'm not kissing you outside the church with all those people watching.*

"I've brought some gob-stoppers along, darling."
Meaning: *Let's try and be a little bit more adventurous tonight.*

"Will it embarrass your parents if we kiss in front of them."
Meaning: *Who cares, here goes.*

"Were there many loves before me?"
Meaning: *Where did you learn to kiss like that?*

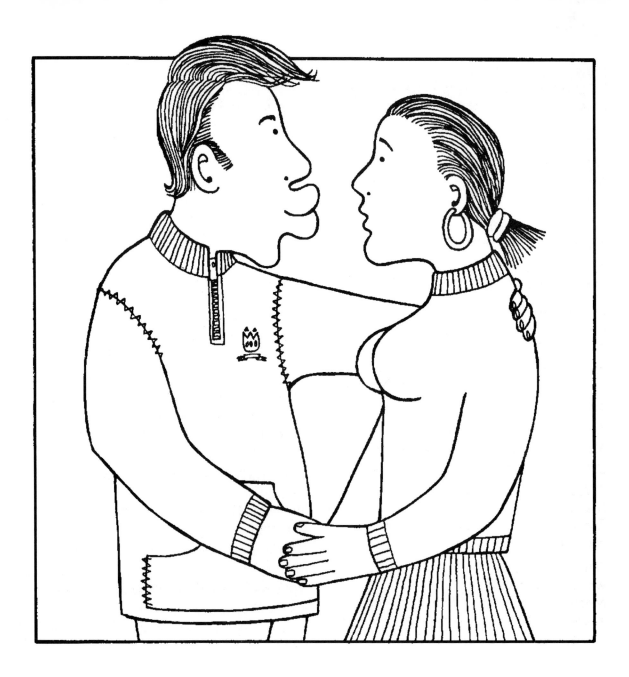

"Kissing you sends me into a total tizzy."
Meaning: *For a few seconds there I couldn't work out whose tongue was whose.*

"Yikes, what was that?!"
Meaning: *Another electric shock.*

"Don't be too vigorous when we kiss dear."
Meaning: *You don't know I've got falsies yet.*

"What striking lip-stick you're wearing dear."
Meaning: *What striking lip-stick I'm about to be wearing.*

"Darling, you're so virile."
Meaning: *Blimey, it's like a jungle by these earlobes.*

"Auntie Bertha, how are you?"
Meaning: *Gulp, here goes, let's hope I can get away with her cheek.*

"Waaaah, waaah, waaaah...."
Meaning: *I may be only six months old but no Tory politician is going to kiss me to win support.*

"Phew, your passion was like a rainstorm when we kissed last night."
Meaning: *Any chance of sucking in and swallowing before we start - I nearly drowned last night.*

"I could eat you alive."
Meaning: *I'll make a start with your upper lip.*

"I could choke on my love for you."
Meaning: *I must try and avoid swallowing her dentures tonight.*

"Your designer stubble makes me go all tingly."
Meaning: *It's also scratching my face to bits."*

"Darling, your lips feel so big and round."
Meaning: *Kissing you is like kissing an over-inflated car tyre. Odds on you've had your lips surgically enhanced by a surgeon who fell asleep on the job.*

"Your lips are so delicate and sensitive, I barely felt them as we kissed."
Meaning: *I was so nervous I pulled away before they touched.*

"Your love for me is like a mysterious and exotic smell from another land."
Meaning: *You had curry again last night, didn't you?*

"I hear wild, deafening music every time we kiss."
Meaning: *Couldn't you take that AC/DC tape out of your walkman for one romantic moment?*

9
Advanced Snogging

Your First Tongue-Sandwich

Somewhere in the course of a kisser's early snogging days - later for some kissers - an important physical discovery is made. Kissing can be done not only with the mouths closed, not only with the mouths open but with bodily communication of a physical nature taking place unbeknown to the outside world inside the mouth.

You may not be able to talk to each other in words mid-snog, but your tongues can talk to each other in the language of love. Welcome to the tongue-sandwich, that peculiarly romantic intercourse of the mouths.

It's fairly straightforward - just put your tongue fairly straight forward.

With a bit of luck you'll find another fat little wet thing tickling your own tickler. Hopefully it's not a nose.

Her First Tongue-Sandwich

Ought to be around the same moment as your own. But if your own tongue is getting excessively waggly and all macho and excited...your partner's may chicken out of a meeting of the minds until you calm down.

> **It was reported in 1991 that a 19-year-old girl had died of a kiss at a party. Apparently she had kissed someone who was carrying a strain of meningitis.**

Exchanging Mouthily Fluids

Researchers have established that every time someone takes a drink from a can of pop, the remaining drink contains 10 per cent saliva. This suggests that after ten people have had a swig, everyone else is cooling their thirst with a can of saliva. Yeuch!

This important research can be translated to the field of the lip-smacker, particularly with reference to Tongue-Waggler Flesh-Chomperitis (as the humble Tongue-Sandwich has come to be known to scientists).

Once you have been snogging for quite a while with the same partner, your body fluids are so mixed up that it's just as well that your hearts are...it'd be very difficult to untangle them again.

Show-Off Snogging: Tricks For Applause

There is an endless variety to the life of the really good snogger, including a lovely collection of tricks to be learnt. But remember: whatever you do, don't try any of these tricks with an adult around.

The Bubble Gum Stickler

Insert a new piece of bubble gum in your mouth prior to starting your snog. Once it is nicely gluey, begin your snog. (Your partner must have done the same.) Now try swapping the gum from one mouth to the other without tangling it or getting it stuck in the mouth from

> **The longest ever underwater kiss is two minutes and 18 seconds.**

which it originally came.

The successful couple will be able to complete their snog by each blowing a post-snog bubble - using the partner's piece of gum.

Swapping Dentures

This is self-explanatory really, but it can be extremely tricky, especially if partners have different sets of original teeth missing. *Warning: only attempt this trick if your relationship is highly stable. It can lead to divorce.*

Underwater

In the bath or in the sea, snogging has a special intimacy when you are reliant on your partner's supply of oxygen to keep alive.

Kiss of Life

A phrase used to describe the saving of another person's life by blowing your own life into them via the vehicle of the humble kiss.

> **Five members of an Australian St John's Ambulance Team gave the kiss of life in 1984 for a record 315 hours to 232,150 patients - inflatable dummies.**

In fact all kissing should be the kissing of life from one person into another, regardless of whether they were dying before or not.

INTERESTING FACT: *When God first made the world, the Bible says He breathed life into it - i.e. He kissed the universe into being.*

"Doing a 360" - 360 Degrees Kissing

One of you lies down, you kiss with your partner at 90 degrees and continue kissing as she moves round you like a clock hand. Only your mouths may be in contact. Twenty seconds and no injuries is considered a good time for a complete lap.

"I hear that kissing breeds disease."
"Let's start an epidemic."

VALENTINE'S MESSAGES

BALDILOCKS - one smile from your crinkly eyes and my hair falls out too, Delilah

BALLERINA, come dance with me P.J

BEANSPROUT, All my love, from the middle-sized-bear

SCRAPPY, Let me share your bone, Love always, Scooby

ALL my love from your loving admirer

ANTHONY, I'll be yours forever, Love Margaret

THE woods are lovely, dark and deep – share my nest with me, love Woodchuck

C.S. Love always P.R

LEO Lion, Let me stroke your mane, Virgo

MIKE, Come back and stay for good this time, Janie

DEAREST Dear, Promise you'll always be here for me Sam xxx

SNOWBALL, miss your hugs and kisssesss Barnaby

ANDYPandy, love...and no strings attached, Looby Loo

DARLING Claire, Happy Valentines day, Joe

BIG BIRD, Let me see your neck dance, Ali

JJ, I love the way you walk round corners, You Know Who

BOB, love always, Kathy

BIG Billy Goat Gruff, Marry me before the Trolls get me!

DARLING Kermit, many choo choos, Miss Piggy

CUDDLESOME, Forgive me, Groper

RM, no complications this time, Sue

PORCUPINE - Owl still loves you

CINDY, Love and kisses, Superman

STEAM PUDDING, Loves custard, X

DEBBIE you're the only one for me, love John

RICK, Remember the Ramada Inn, Raleigh? Love B x

BOOP, I Love you, Monster munch

FUZZYBEAR, All my love, Chunky chicken

YAHOO, make it Swift, Cucumber

CHARMER, Try not to charm anyone while I'm away, Back soon, miss you, Mimi

DOUGAL, Love's Magic second time around, Love Florence

CANDY, Big Happy Valentines Day, Big Love, Pete

POOH, I love you more each day, Piglet

BEANIE, you're still the best, Cuddlette

CLAIRE, I love you, Stan

THUNDER thighs, Be mine, The Beast

BRAZIL, nuts about you, Pecan

NEIL, For a forest boy you've got a nice butt, love always Debs

MRS BADGER, with all my undying love, Mr Badger

TOBY, I love your big one, love Lucy

ROSIE B, Tonight's the night. Remember me.

MICHAEL, You're my dream boy, love Chloe

MARK, you've got yourself a British Souvenir! XX

STEVE, my Valentine forever, TT

ROSES are red, violets are blue, its been 10 years and I still love you

PORKY, love you, Bacon

MARK, lots of love Joanne

MARTY, I'd travel the world with you, kiss you at the station, love Ginny

KEN, lots of love, Dierdre X

PIGGY Wiggy, Remember the good times from your very own Prince

P.E. Position me

MARK, When I am sad and weary, When I feel all hope has gone, I walk along Fulham Palace Road and think of you with nothing on, Ami

RICHARD, I never knew,
Till I saw you
How great a love can be,
But now you're here,
I hold you near
You are a part of me, Susan

ZOE, Up the ladder 1,2,3
If you fall, fall for me, Michael

TWEEDLEDEE searching for Tweedledum, phone after tea time

ROMEO, Let me be your Juliet

BROWNEYE, I love you

SQUIRREL who needs the rest I've got the best, Ratty

BUNNYKINS can't wait until Friday, wear the marmalade, M

Homogenous Zones

The Body (In Briefs)

HIM

Ear Lobes
Often nibbled by courting couples. Warning: bite too hard and they come off in your mouth. End of relationship.

Nose
Keep it clean, eh?

Nasal hair
Can be unruly. If it's long pop it in a pony tail for tidiness.

Upper Lip
Found just above lower lip, best used in conjunction.

Neck
Can be used in conjunction with lips. Hence phrase "necking". Dangerous on the easily aroused but fun. Love-bites often placed here.

Nipple
Unclear what they are for on a man. Babies like to kiss them on their mums - giving them their first kissing experience.

Censored Box See next book.

Eyebrows
Watch them if you want to keep them. Some amorous kissers can get carried away - and start plucking them from you mid-clinch with their teeth.

Chests, Hairy
Commonly believed to be romantic, usually if they are on the man.

Chest, Bald
Other women prefer not to go sniffing in your body-hair but find a smooth, bronzed chest exciting. You may like to keep your options open by shaving half your chest regularly.

Chest, Rug
Useful romantic accessory if you just can't get those hairs to move around from your forearm and come out on your chest.

Knee Cap
One found on most legs and often used to lean on and balance body in act of folding down on one knee to make proposal of marriage.

(And how to get them)

& HER

Hair
If hair is long and floppy, can get easily caught up and tangled in partner's lips, ruining kiss-sensation. Keep carefully tied back until serious passion unfolds - then fling hairband, with caution, to winds.

Back of hand
May be offered to you by your lady friend, in which case you should either kiss it discreetly and with humility or duck because she is about to slap you in the chops.

Hand
Ideal for everything from the romantic clinch to the big sloppy hug to the cheeky squeeze of the funny bits.

Ankles
Found at junction between leg and foot but not generally an historical kissable area on the male form. Often highly kissable on the female form, especially in eastern cultures. Warning: Don't get your teeth caught in the ankle band.

Teeth
Use to nibble partner's ear lobes or other erogenous bits.
Warning: falsies can embarrass.

Shoulders
If your partner is tired, fed up and got a headache after a tough day down at the slaughterhouse, why not try a gentle rubbing session with your firm hands (see earlier) - known in the trade as a "massage" - which can often work wonders. If the hands fail, a bite may do the trick.

Breasts
For breast-feeding of course. See **Nipple** above.

Finger
For engagement ring, when the time is right. In the words of the song by Martha Reeves and The Vandellas, "Third finger, left hand" - don't get it wrong.

Finger
For wedding ring when time is right. Don't forget it.

10
Going All The Way - Marriage

The expression "going all the way" has come to have a distinctly sexual connotation, referring to that climactic moment of physical intimacy in a snogging couple's relationship.

But as the authors of this book are of a more traditionalist bent in matters of sexual mores, they will be using it in the sense of its original meaning - "going all the way up the aisle", getting hitched, being wedded, tying the knot, throwing in your lot, calling it a day, etc.

> My boyfriend and I broke up, he wanted to get married, I didn't want him to.
>
> *Rita Rudner*

(*Apologies to those readers who were expecting this section to update that important landmark publication, The Joy of Sex - just not that kind of book and anyway men don't wear those kind of funny beards any more. Not even on their chins.*)

When to Consider Going All The Way

Of course it varies for different couples but a rough principle would be after the first date and before thirty-five years have passed.

Somewhere in there you should both get the feeling that you were made for each other or that you were specifically made for anyone but each other - in which case it's not worth

going all the way. (One common time in which couples consider getting married is if one or other or both have "fallen" pregnant. This indicates that you have done a little more than snogging - although there are people around who believe that even snogging should be confined to the marriage bed for the simple reason that it can lead to pregnancy if practised too passionately. This unusual view is not thought to be scientifically verifiable and is not generally accepted in medical circles - or any other circles we can think of. Except perhaps The Magic Circle....)

Suffice to say that a good time to consider marriage is not on on your first night out...or your second, third, fourth etc.... Take your time. Despite all the feelings to the contrary in the middle of another spine-tingling-snog, the world is not going to end just yet....

How to know for sure

Impossible. You can't. If you wait till you're 100% certain you'll never get anywhere, you'll also become a very boring person. Make a list of all the qualities you expect in a life-long partner. Alongside write a list of your intended's qualities - do they match? Of course they don't. Welcome to the real world!

Here are some points to look out for.

1. If they can snog you after a seriously spicy curry, you'd be a fool to pass on them. Even though it may pass on you.

2. If she sees you at your worst - i.e. first thing in the morning on the landing with gunge on your lips, sleep in your eyes, bad breath and bad taste pyjamas - and she still fancies a snog, this is the real thing mate.

3. She's got more money than you.

4. Picture her in fifty years, firm bits gone saggy, glasses, varicose veins, large underwear...you'll probably go well together. Except she'll have more hair.

5. Large area of overlap in your record collection: this is good and indicates an important degree of cultural unity...until you have to decide whose copy of which record is kept.

Meeting the in-laws

Her in-laws shouldn't be a problem. They're your parents. Then again....

Proposing

Can be done as the ad says, "Any time, any place, anywhere" - time and again though, creativity has proved to be the key. One knee and the ring is fine but predictable. Try any of the following, highly original proposals....

1. Jeremy Peters and Les Lyons met at a Magic Convention and fell in love. When Jeremy popped the question, he produced the ring by regurgitating it from his bowel in mid-clinch. (On second thoughts, don't try this one.)

2. Keen footballer Stephen Bainbridge, of

> In 1989 the *Daily Mirror* newspaper reported that queuing up to kiss the bride at a wedding reception could damage your health. But the nearer you are to the front of the queue the less risk you take.
>
> Acording to the medical journal *The Lancet*, you could catch something nasty via the bride's lips from somebody who kissed her earlier. But a simple answer was suggested: - wiping the bride's cheek with a tissue before kissing her. Ideally the tissue should be soaked in antiseptic first, suggested one doctor.
>
> So don't forget a bottle of antiseptic and some tissues next time you're off to a wedding.

> You don't know a woman till you've met her in court.
>
> *Norman Mailer*

Kirkaldy in Fife, arranged to be fouled right in front of his beloved. She rushed onto the pitch behind the manager who, of course, had the magic sponge and bucket...except it turned out to be a champagne bucket complete with sparkling champagne and diamond ring. Aaaaaah!

3. Natalie Greenaway of Boston, Massachusets, got so fed up of waiting for boyfriend James "Snailpace" Patterson to propose to her that she bought him a jeweller's. The whole shop, plus stock. "I just said, 'Choose one, any one, I know I'll like it, they're all mine anyway...'."

Inspired yet, try these....

4. Bill McShane of Detroit got a skywriter to spell out "I love you Jill, Marry me..." in half-mile high letters above his girlfriend's house. But the writing was so bad Jill thought it said, "Hove, you're still mammy"
She ignored it...and him.

5. Felix Trabatori, from Milan, bought his fiancée one hundred beautiful red and white roses - in the middle of this spectacular horticultural arrangement was a note declaring undying love and a proposal of marriage. She never got that far. While enjoying the stunning fragrance of the flowers, she had a savage asthma attack and died. (Perhaps you'd better not try this one either.)

Actually Popping The Question

Visit the local bookie, get them to quote you odds on a successful proposition. Bet heavily against yourself. This way, if you fail, at least you will have covered your expenses.

Don't be too bold and self-confident, she might think you've done it before. In fact try to appear slightly embarrassed and somewhat flustered. Some women find this cute and endearing.

Work out how she may react. Cover all possiblities. Don't be surprised by a "No", a "Yes", a "Maybe", a "What's the Catch?" or an "Only if you stop eating that spring onion".

If she says "Yes", you must try and ensure your eyes immediately fill with tears, that you choke on something as you say "Thank you Tooth Fairy, wherever you are."

If she says "No", you must try and ensure your eyes fill with tears, and you choke on something as you say, "You're paying the bill, you maggot."

Avoid these phrases at all costs

So how about it then?
I prefer Mrs to Ms don't you?
I pledge thee my troth...(*whoever wanted their pledge trothed anyway?*)

> **Marriage is a wonderful invention - but then so is the bicycle repair kit.**
> **Billy Connolly**

I've always wanted six boys...
A season ticket is cheaper for two...
I've already booked the Masons' Hall...

Where and How To Get Married

The Advantages of a Church Ceremony

People think this is the way that weddings are "done properly".
It can be a nice setting...if the building is in reasonable nick.
The video is more interesting. (Deadly all the same.)
At least the reception doesn't have to be all religious.
It seems more "real" than a registry office.

The Advantages of a Registry Office Ceremony

It's over much quicker.
You don't have a dull vicar warbling on for ever while everyone's thinking about confetti and whether the reception is any good.

> **A man in love is incomplete until he has married - then he's finished.**
> **Zsa Zsa Gabor**

The town hall is probably better placed for bus services for guests.
The video is shorter.

Choosing a Photographer

Undoubtedly one of the worst parts of every wedding. The worst suit coupled with the least sincere smile will always belong to the photographer.
Listen out for his catch phrases and applaud them as they come up:
That's Lovely...
 Smashing...
Come on, Gran, give us your best smile...
Who's that joker at the back...?
Just the brides's family, please.
Can someone keep him still?
NO CONFETTI YET.
Where's the garter?

> **A wedding is just a happy funeral.**
> **Paul Theroux**

> **"You wanna know the secret of life?" asked Tony Curtis, the actor. "The saliva of young girls."**

Just one more?
Please NO CONFETTI!
Could I have everyone on?
Just one more...
Shall I take some tonight, eh ?(*nudge, nudge, what a joker*)
Just one more...
Oh No, there's no film in it...just kidding, ha ha...(*what a joker*)

Whether to Invite the Family

You better had, they'll find out anyway. And if you don't, it's bound to cause a row.

The Big Night

Don't forget clean socks.

Snogging all over the World

No matter where in the world you live there is a simple rule that people have found helpful down the years. If you see two people with their tongues down each other's throats they quite like each other.

This apart, it is important to understand the cultural differences that make snogging around the world such a diverse and educational hobby.

Swaziland

A marriage is not deemed valid in Swaziland until a public embrace has consisted of at least 100 kisses - because the King has hundreds of wives. Quite how many no one knows. Not even His Majesty. Some couples are so enthusiastic that this can go on all day. One couple who started in 1987 are still going.

> **A delectable gal from Augusta,**
> **Vowed that nobody ever had bussed her**
> **But an expert from France**
> **Took a bilingual chance**
> **And the mixture of tongues quite non-plussed her.**
> **Conrad Aiken, 1965**

> **Flirt: a woman who thinks it's every man for herself.**
> **Anon**

Australia

Group-kissing has caught on in parts of Brisbane and Adelaide to such a degree that sales of lip-moisturiser have rocketed. The basic idea is that when you see a couple kissing, you and your partner approach from opposite sides, get down to their head-height and try to kiss each other through the other couple's lips. Not healthy but great fun.

Japan

Part of ancestral worship which is common-place in Japan, starts with deep respect for grandparents. This means kissing them regularly. Far too regularly. Unlikely to catch on here.

Switzerland

Swiss fruit bats have a bizarre and involved mating ritual which involves slow head rotations which speed up as the two bodies approach. As they finally meet - a process

which can take anything up to eight hours - head rotations increase to mind-boggling speeds. As a result of this, the Swiss have what they call a bat-kiss which involves clockwise head movement and anti-clockwise tongue movement. Difficult to maintain for more than five seconds without general hysteria.

Germany

If you ever get invited to a "Munich Banquet" beware. You certainly have very fine food and wines but it is passed to you not on plates but via someone else's mouth - the general idea being that by the time it has gone down a line of twelve or so diners, the flavour has been

> **One survey in the early 1980s revealed that in London, 59% of people kiss on the lips each day but in Scotland only 38% do.**

> **We don't believe in rheumatism and true love until after the first attack.**
> *Marie Ebner von Eschenbach*

improved somewhat by additions from your eating partners. Not strictly kissing but we just thought you'd like to know.

Greenland

For obvious reasons kissing is almost exclusively an indoor experience here, but supposedly one of the best available. This is because a Greenlander's body over-compensates for the devastating cold that surrounds them and produces the hottest saliva in the world. Kissing in Greenland is apparently like snogging a boiling kettle. Ouch!

Later that night...

The Big Snog...

(see next book)

CONFESSIONS

*We're sorry, we wouldn't have eaten
Uncle Eric if we'd known ...*

*It was my mum's prize mynah bird that
I accidentally hoovered up ...*

*I didn't think that all the people on the escalator
would actually fall off when it stopped*

For thousands of people who would never darken the door of a church.
Simon Mayo's *Confessions* slot on Radio One's Breakfast Show has provided the
perfect opportunity for off-loading guilt and clearing consciences.

An amazing catalogue of sins has been paraded before a listening public of
up to eleven million people every day and forgiveness begged from
'Father' Mayo and the Breakfast Crew.

The seven deadly sins (and dozens more besides) are all here:
the best of the worst of human nature.